Saying What You Mean

A Children's Book about Communication Skills

by

Joy Wilt

Illustrated by Ernie Hergenroeder

Educational Products Division
Word, Incorporated
Waco, Texas

Author

JOY WILT is creator and director of Children's Ministries, an organization that provides resources "for people who care about children"—speakers, workshops, demonstrations, consulting services, and training institutes. A certified elementary school teacher, administrator, and early childhood specialist, Joy is also consultant to and professor in the master's degree program in children's ministries for Fuller Theological Seminary. Joy is a graduate of LaVerne College, LaVerne, California (B.A. in Biological Science), and Pacific Oaks College, Pasadena, California (M.A. in Human Development). She is author of two books, *Happily Ever After* and *An Uncomplicated Guide to Becoming a Superparent,* as well as the popular *Can-Make-And-Do Books.* Joy's commitment "never to forget what it feels like to be a child" permeates the many innovative programs she has developed and her work as lecturer, consultant, writer, and—not least—mother of two children, Christopher and Lisa.

Artist

ERNIE HERGENROEDER is owner and operator of Hergie & Associates (an advertising agency and graphics production house). His desire to draw came at the early age of three, and all through high school he achieved top honors in art. In 1961 he joined the United States Air Force, and became the Wing Commander's personal illustrator. From 1965 to 1975 he owned and operated a successful sign company in Sonora, California. In 1975 he sold his business in order to devote his full attention to drawing cartoons. Ernie, his wife Faith, and their four children Lynn, Kathy, Stephen, and Beth now reside in San Jose, California.

Saying What You Mean

Contents

Introduction

<u>Saying What You Mean</u> is one of a series of books. The complete set is called ***Ready-Set-Grow!***

<u>Saying What You Mean</u> deals with communication skills and can be used by itself or as a part of a program that utilizes all of the ***Ready-Set-Grow!*** books.

<u>Saying What You Mean</u> is specifically designed for children four to eight years of age. A child can either read the book or have it read to him or her. This can be done at home, church, or school.

<u>Saying What You Mean</u> is designed to involve the child in the concepts that are being taught. This is done by simply and carefully explaining each concept and then asking questions that invite a response from the child. It is hoped that by answering the questions the child will personalize the concept and, thus, integrate it into his or her thinking.

Many problems and conflicts that arise in human relationships can be attributed to a "lack of communication." Poor communication often results from not understanding what communication is. For this reason, Saying What You Mean carefully defines and explains both verbal and nonverbal communication.

Saying What You Mean also strives to teach children how to communicate effectively. It teaches them that what one says will best be communicated when it is said at the right time to the right people in the right way. Saying What You Mean clearly outlines what constitutes the "right time," the "right people," and the "right way" so that children can begin to control what they say and how it is received.

Saying What You Mean is designed to teach a child that God created him or her with the ability to communicate. Communicating is part of God's plan for every person. Children who grow up learning good, positive communication skills will be better equipped to develop and maintain productive relationships.

God created you a person, and because you are one,

you are a communicator.

9

You began being a communicator when you were a baby.

When you were hungry, you cried. Your cry communicated that you wanted something to eat.

When you were tired, you yawned and rubbed your eyes. Your yawn and sleepy eyes communicated that you needed to sleep.

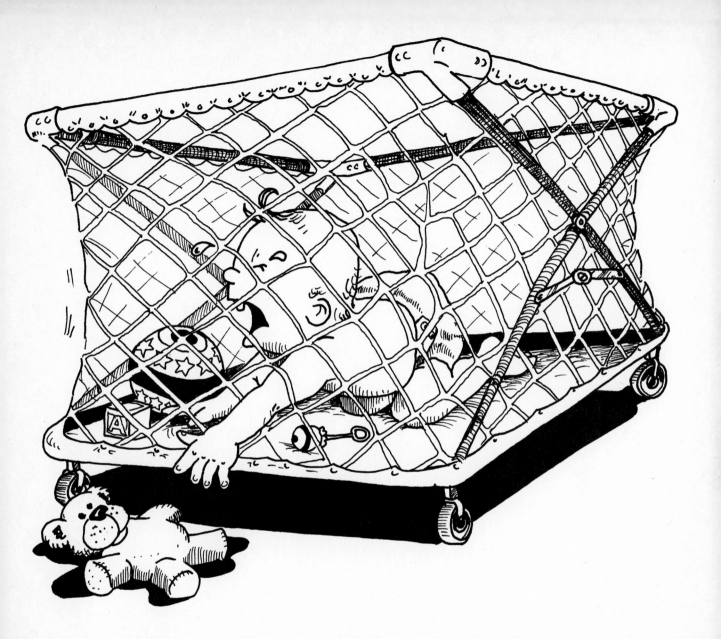

When you were uncomfortable or frustrated, you fussed and whined. Your fussing and whining communicated that you needed help and attention.

When you were happy and content, you smiled, giggled, and cooed.

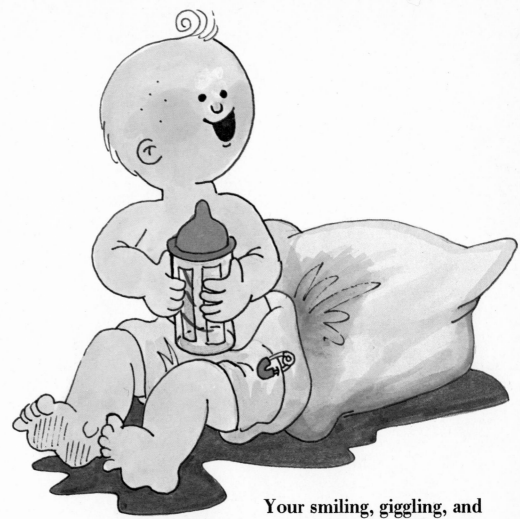

Your smiling, giggling, and cooing communicated that you liked whatever was happening and the way everything was at that moment.

Although you did not say any words, you communicated. From the very beginning of your life, you were a communicator.

Communication is exchanging or passing along feelings, thoughts, or information.

A communicator is one who exchanges or passes along feelings, thoughts, or information.

You are a communicator.
You communicate every day with everyone around you.
You communicate in many ways.

Chapter 1

Communicating with Your Body

Sometimes you use your head to communicate. . .

"Yes."

"No."

Sometimes you use your face to communicate. . .

"I'm happy."

"I'm sad."

Your face can communicate. . .

"I'm mad."

"I'm annoyed and frustrated."

Your face can communicate. . .

"I'm thinking."

"I'm confused."

Your face can communicate. . .

"I'm surprised!"

"I'm worried."

Your face can communicate. . .

"I'm scared."

"I'm disappointed."

Sometimes you use your hands to say. . .

"No."

"OK."

Your hands can say...

"I hope so."

"Two."

Your hands can say. . .

"Shhh. That's too loud."

"I can't hear."

Sometimes you use your arms and hands to communicate...

"Hello and good-bye."

"Over there."

Your arms and hands can say. . .

"You."

"Me."

Your arms and hands can say. . .

"Give it to me."

"Take it."

Your arms and hands can say. . .

"Come here."

"Stay away."

Your arms and hands can say. . .

"I don't know."

"I won!"

Your arms and hands can say. . .

"You did a good job! I liked what you did!"

"Let's be friends."

Sometimes your whole body can communicate. . .

"I love you."

"I hate you."

Your body can say. . .

"I'm shy. Leave me alone."

"I feel rejected and alone."

Your body can say. . .

"I'm confident. I know I can do it."

"I'm proud of myself. I like the things I do."

You are a communicator.
You communicate every day with everyone around you.

You use your

    head,
    face,
    hands,
    arms,

    and whole body to communicate.

Chapter 2

Communicating with Art, Music, Dance, Writing, and Drama

Sometimes you communicate through art.

WATERCOLOR PAINT SET

Sometimes you communicate through music.

Sometimes you communicate
by dancing.

Sometimes you communicate by writing.

66

Sometimes you communicate through drama.

You are a communicator.
You communicate every day with everyone around you.

You can communicate through:

        art,
        music,
        dance,
        writing, or
        drama.

Chapter 3

Communicating with Words

Talking is another way you communicate.

When you talk, you use words.

Sometimes you need only one word to communicate.

Words like hello
        yes
        no
        stop
        go
        wait
        O K
        look
        please
        thanks
        sorry, and
        don't   . . . are sometimes all you need
                                  to communicate everything
                                  you want to communicate.

At other times, you need more than one word to communicate.

Words are only letters of the alphabet put together.

What you do with words, how you put them together and how you say them, makes them a form of communication.

What you do with Words...

The same words can communicate different messages.

The meaning you give to words depends upon many
things, such as. . .

how softly or. . .

how loudly you say them.

The meaning you give to words depends upon. . .

how fast you say them.

The meaning you give to words depends upon. . .

how unkindly you say them.

The meaning you give to words depends upon. . .

85

DO YOU THINK YOU CAN DO IT?

YES!

The meaning you give to
words depends upon. . .

how confidently or . . .

86

how timidly you say them.

The meaning you give to words depends upon. . .

how enthusiastically or . . .

how unenthusiastically you say them.

The meaning you give to words depends upon. . .

what you are doing. . .

when you say them.

You are a communicator.
You communicate every day with everyone around you.
You can communicate by saying words:

> softly or loudly,
> slow or fast,
> kindly or unkindly,
> sincerely or insincerely,
> confidently or timidly,
> enthusiastically or unenthusiastically.

You can communicate by reinforcing the words you
say with what you do.

Chapter 4

Communicating What You Want to Communicate

(Saying What You Mean)

Sometimes you want to communicate to someone how you feel.

Sometimes you want to communicate to someone what you think.

Sometimes you want to communicate to someone what you want.

Sometimes you want to communicate to someone what you need.

Sometimes you want to communicate to someone
your hopes and dreams.

Sometimes you want to communicate to someone facts and information.

If you want to communicate important things like

    how you feel,
    what you think,
    what you want,
    what you need,
    your hopes and dreams,   or
    facts and information,

        . . . you need to do several things.

To begin with, important things need to be communicated at the right time.

It is not the right time to communicate important things...

if the person you want to communicate with is
too busy to think about what you are saying.

You need to wait for a time when you can communicate.

MOM, I'M NOT BUSY NOW. CAN YOU TALK?

You need to wait for a time when the person you
want to communicate with can listen, and then. . .

Communicate!

Second, important things need to be communicated
to the right people.

People who are not interested in you are not the
right people to whom you should communicate
important things.

People who are not interested in what you are saying are not the right people to whom you should communicate important things.

You need to find someone who is interested in you.

You need to find someone who is interested in
what you have to say, and then. . .

Communicate!

Third, important things need to be communicated accurately and honestly.

This boy's communication. . .

is accurate and honest.

This boy's communication is not accurate and honest.

This girl's communication. . .

is accurate and honest.

This girl's communication is not accurate ? and honest.

I HATE BABIES! THEY CRY TOO MUCH!

is accurate and honest.

This boy's communication is not accurate and honest.

Only when you communicate accurately and honestly can people know and understand what you want them to know and understand. Only when you communicate accurately and honestly can people respond accurately and honestly to you.

Before you communicate,
  think about what you are going to say.

Then, say it   as accurately

122

and as honestly as you can.

You are a communicator.
You communicate every day with everyone around you.
When you communicate important things, remember to:

communicate at the right time,
communicate to the right people, and
communicate accurately and honestly.

Conclusion

God created you a person, and because you are one, you are a communicator.

Good communication will help you get along
with other people. It can make your life happier.

Good communication all depends on how well you. . .

Say what you mean.